Take the "ick" out of THick INK!

Marianne Moffat Rowbotham

Take the "ick" out of THick INK!
Copyright © 2020 by Marianne Moffat Rowbotham

All rights reserved. No part of this publication may be reproduced, distributed, or transmitted in any form or by any means, including photocopying, recording, or other electronic or mechanical methods, without the prior written permission of the author, except in the case of brief quotations embodied in critical reviews and certain other non-commercial uses permitted by copyright law.

Tellwell Talent
www.tellwell.ca

ISBN
978-0-2288-3077-1 (Paperback)

Table of Contents

To My Mom 1
I'll thank thee if the meal be good; 2
Arts or Science – The Big Question 3
To Work at Home or Not 4
L'ordinateur is my very clean pencil; 7
I'd like to invite the women home -- 8
Reality impinges 9
Thank thee for my body. 10
I was having a Gup of Goffee 11
The gift of meat, my Lord. 12
The sky is a myriad of cloud formations 13
If I should be …. 14
… For Cooking is the Strong Art. 15
O we thank Thee for the Blood 16
To Brian. 17
In the morning, ... 19
Fatigue 22
Who to Support – NASA or the Church? 23
Am I a witch? 25
Magnifichat. 27
Mary still needs that stable 29
I'll be your little lap-dog, God 30
Astronomy 32
Eau, sacred eau 35
Do you want me, O God 36
I took this course for something to do, ... 38
Walking down these hallowed halls of learning 39
A Homemaker's Spring Song 40
On the 'Windows' Tutorial 42

You can	43
The solution to boredom is creativity.	44
Gotta have my Goffee	45
This is a new day,	48
You've got to believe	49
I Sewed Him a Name-Tag	50
Hair Loss	52
Coffee	53
Torture	54
No Fire Today	55
An Early Valentine – "The Kept Wife"	57
Beginning	59
O Dream that will not let me go	61
God! Why inflame me with desire	64
Oh Lord, Thou art too far away.	67
God has been with me	68
Morning Visions	70
Morning has come,	71
Last night I dreamt I was true to You	72
"There will be a job for me	73
Fowl Supper	74
Freeze Frame #1	75
The rays of the sun say "Run."	76
Where is God in All This?	78
He didn't even notice	80
This Music thing	81
Ode to the Cow	83
Safe Landing	86
Prayer for the Junior Choir	88
Naïve?	89
6:40 a.m.	91
The wind is like a furbelow	92
Halcrow Marsh	93
Chez moi	*94*
If there were a Planet	95

Pray a reverent prayer on Christmas Eve	97
We have a private bedroom	98
How can I express	99
A poem for you,	100
In fourteen hundred and ninety-two	102
Autumn Song	103
Thank Thee for my body.	104
The gift of meat, my Lord	105
God was the Word,	106
Secretary or French Teacher?	107
Dear God, I thank you for my life.	109
I've just got up; dawn's grey light is near.	110
3 January, 2000 A.D.	112
Holy Communion in the United Church of Canada	114
Each brain is a garden	115
He, She or Thee	117
Who can comprehend little boys	118
We are not afraid.	119
In the morning.	121
Everything's revealed again –	124
I say to the blue,	125
On Thanksgiving.	126
The sky is cerulean blue,	127
The colours are not harsh	128
The wind sighs,"No!",	129
It's wonderful!	130
Prayer for the Life of my Seeds	131
It's that wonderful, tremulous time	132
A November Poem	133
The sky is too blue, the sun too bright	134
Start your day with a pencil.	135
'Though on the one hand I love you	136
It's a Miracle	139
Oh God	140
My love affair with the pencil and pen	141

I must take in words	142
God uses His agent, the Sun	143
Raisins and almonds are food for the Jew.	144
A Grace Before Dinner	147
Before it was so clear	148
I'm married to a man both gentle and strong.	150
I know that I'm not stupid	151
Here's to the kids	152
Untitled — Undated	153
There is something about today	155
What you see is what you see	156
O woodpecker	157
Morning Coffee	158
Sing to the Lord a New Song	159
Hurrah for Herb Teas!	161
Wake up, my eyes –	162
The god of garbage looks askance;	163
Humble, pastel, faded napkins	164
It's a good day.	165
Slam goes the door	166
Christ died that we might live.	167
O	170
Inspiration from Somewhere on a Sleepless Night	171
Ideas are so wonderful –	172
He, She or Thee	173
Night of Innocence	175
Read an article	176
Sun Rising	177
On My Birthday	178
Dashing through the snow	179
The Pencil	180
The sky is a myriad of cloud formations	182
O we thank Thee for the Blood	183
Prediction	184

1.   March 28, 1998

To My Mom

While you're away,
I miss you.
No one else will do.
And so in my heart
I kiss you,
And wait till your holiday's through.
I know you are fine and well-cared-for;
I know there's no reason to phone,
But I just want to bless you
And show you you're not alone.

2. Dec. 16, 2002

I'll thank thee if the meal be good;
If not, I'll play Robin Hood —
Put it in an appropriate place
In my Filing System space,
To a different species, give,
Or in the Compost let it live.

3. April 1, 2001

Arts or Science – The Big Question

Two alternate paths
For our youth –
Two important ways
To aid the truth –
Making every tongue a bilingual one –
Or finding another useful Sun –
Seeker of Friendship or Seeker of Stars –
Which is it <u>most</u> that you really are?

4. June 26, 1994

To Work at Home or Not

Is it write or is it rong?
Am I the singer or the song?
Am I the heroine or the maid?
The maker of peace or the country betrayed?
Is it write or is it type?
These hands that can see a human face,
And sketch it fairly true,
These hands that reproduce the notes
And <u>mood</u>
If they are willing to,
These hands that can take whole-grain flour
And sculpt a corpse for Bread,
These hands that can stitch neatly
Or snip recalcitrant thread,
These that will fiercely cut
If that is what God said –

Striking machine keys
At high velocities
To reproduce numbers and letters
"If you please"
Is a job, not a pleasure,
A race to be won,
Great effort to trap the cheese.

Our goal will be to increase our worth
To see the numbers rise
Instead of watching the living yeast
Increase the bread-dough's size.

But is it both-and
Or is it either-or --
Maybe if we hire a <u>cook</u>
Not just someone to wash floor?
Kraft dinner is so swift and cheap
Instant almost 'nuff,
With quick-fry animal
And other freeze-dried "stuff".
With minimal preparation
And severe control
I may drag myself
Out of the kitchen "hole".

But I can't go to sew
If I must type.
That is rong.
It isn't <u>write</u>.

5.   October '94

L'ordinateur is my very clean pencil;
L'ordinateur helps me go where it's at;
Here is a place to sharpen fingernails:
A computer keyboard's the chair for a cat.

6. October '94

(to the tune of "I'd like to buy the world a Coke")

I'd like to invite the women home --
Let them see how nice it is,
Let them feel quiet in their hearts
Away from all the biz.

7.   April 2, 1998

Reality impinges
It gets in the way
Of what I would say to Thee
Oh long, laborious day!

8.   May 14, 1994

Thank thee for my body.
Please be in my soul.
Keep us sane and strong and true
To Thee, O perfect whole.

9.   May 23, 1995

I was having a Gup of Goffee
And I chanced to look real deep
'Thought I saw Lord Jesus Christ --
Gee, thought He was asleep.

I was drinking café au lait
And I chanced to look inside.
Thought I saw my Lord, the Christ.
What a funny place to hide.

10. Dec. 20, 1995

The gift of meat, my Lord
Is more than I can bear.
I know that I must eat it,
Just as I breathe air.

Its taste is so delicious;
It gives me strength to move.
To do without would be
A stroke of sacrificial love.

To be honest, I like it.
It's wonderful to me.
It helps me do the things I do.
It helps me see.

Teach me, Lord, to do without
Those sugary treats
Rather than the vital, good,
And strengthening meat.

11.   April 23, 2000

The sky is a myriad of cloud formations
Permeated by the spiking rays
Of the determined sun,
Like me,
Unwilling to say Adieu
To a day
Not only of spring,
Not only Sunday,
But Easter …
And therefore
I understand, sun,
Why even the truculent clouds
Can't darken you.

12.   Oct. 26, 1991

If I should be ….

Oh little me …

If I should be

the chosen

to bear a child

Alisha,

That Love will be unfrozen,

I do accept

And pray

That such a thing may come to be:

I know that God is ruler now

And will always be.

Life disappears

And reappears.

Cycle goes on forever.

We have waited thousands of years.

May the new ones be <u>clever</u>!

13.

… For Cooking is the Strong Art
And Cutting settles Rage.
This is the Truth to carry Man
From Age to brand new Age.

14.

O we thank Thee for the Blood
And we thank Thee for the mud,
And we wish that we could really speak Thy Name
On a Tuesday or a Wednesday
Or a Monday or a Saturday
As if every day was just the same.

But Sunday is the Holy Day,
When we may talk of Things
That don't relate, adhere to money,
In this flowing world,
This land of milk and honey.

15. Dec. 7, 1992

To Brian

Your woebegone face
Tugs at my heart.
How I wish I could understand
the roots of your sadness
and pull them out --
the pencil marks of your worry
and erase them --
the reasons for anxiety
and excise them.

I can give you myself,
My gifts, my talents, my dreams,
My love,
Our children.

If I could give you Peace,
I would.
If I could give you a jillion gold coins on a silver platter,
I would.
If I could give you an antelope to ride to work on,
I would.
If I could order the sun to beam on you all year round,
I would.

If only I had time to knit you a rainbow!

16. July 26, 1996

In the morning,
When one wakes up
After a dutiful prayer,
There is water;
There is light;
There is air.

And in these times so advanced,
One can compute.
So much to be thankful for –
That you can't refute.

Why pine for rainbows in the sky
Under other suns?
Why hope for costly changes
That might not e'en be fun?

Why should I long for schools,
When office life
Might be perfect
For this wife?
"Minor degenerative changes"
In this leg of mine
Decree that I find a job
Where sitting will be fine.

The cross I bear
Of a vanished dream
Will not make me
Curse or scream.

The children of the future
Are all my hope and aim;
Preserving Mother Earth for them
Is an important game.

More vital than cards
Or golf
Is the vanquishing
Of self.

To leave for the kids
This water, this air --
To slow down pollution <u>everywhere</u>.

To be like my mother,
Without her tobacco,
Is a goal I will pursue ---
And the time I spent chasing vain past
Is time that I would rue.

17. August 1, 1994

Fatigue

I am this piece of paper;
I could be crushed by a paperweight.
I am thin as a feather,
A cloud of gauze
In the universe.

How came I to be so ungrounded?
It is the eternal indoorsness,
The breath of stale air,
The weak apathy of limbs
Unwilling to take burdens.
It is a reaction of fatigue --
The most thorough kind,
The type that numbs
Both body and mind.

18.   August 13, 1994

Who to Support – NASA or the Church?

Christmas

Is the stepping-stone,

The stepping-stone to Heaven,

The slippery rock

We must not fail to grasp

With tender toes

In spite of

Struggle

& cash-register splash --

For if we hold this link

In the chain to the past,

Surely the chain will hold us safe

Over the chasm

To the star –

But the stars are <u>real</u>
And energy's <u>dear</u>
As dear as it can be,
So two divergent paths we take,
The one that comforts,
The one that shakes.

19.   Fall 1994

Am I a witch?
Silhouetted on the moon –
I'll fly far away, wait and see.
A broom will become
A space shuttle
And I'll be on it, wait and see.

Two hundred years from now
My descendants will have coffee and listen
To reports from the Earth they've left behind –
They'll relax in their Lycra shorts
And they'll remember the Earthlings,
The ones who carried the flame,
The ones who squeezed their own dreams
Into the pulsating thundering train,
Into the maelstrom, reaching the current,
Struggling to hear sounds of Land,
Attentive to detail,
Alive to cautions,
Weaving a precious strand.

Alone, yet together,
United by hope,
Each fighting their own personal Devil –
The Devil's name Guilt –
While the Saviour's name's hushed,
As if it had no power against Evil –

(The definition of "witch" is "one who does not believe in God".)

20.   September 4, 1994

Magnifichat

Luckier am I
Than other girls;
Even 'though
I haven't got curls.

I am prettier,
Smarter and healthier
Than any girl I've seen,
Except of course,
Our gracious Queen.

Stop me if I'm wrong
But I think I've got a song
That'll last for an eon,
'Cause I've been dreamin'
in the realm
of science <u>and</u> fiction,
in logic <u>and</u> beauty
in earth <u>and</u> sky.
I've been asking "Why?"

My gratitude exceeds all bounds –
Explodes at the edges –
Imploding it is cancerous
Exploding it's lascivious,
Makes sexual wedges –
I don't care –
CANADA's fair –
We're all considered human
Until we prove otherwise.

My gratitude has an avenue!
In musical finger,
Artistic mouth,
Paper & pencil,
Especially a pen.
Oh! Give me the freedom to live again…
And again… and again!

21. November 1994

Mary still needs that stable
She still dreads the stranger –
She still prays that Someone Strong
Will guide her to a manger.

Starlight twinkle,
Starlight dim --
Foil the nicotine.
Bring Astronauts some meat -
And caviar - and cream.

Shine upon each camera lens
And each telescope.
We've got to find Elusive Star
And its planet Hope.

Long ago the Wisemen
Were given such a beacon;
O Miracle-provider –
The Nations all are speaking!

22.   October 20, 1994

I'll be your little lap-dog, God
Just bring me the coffee.
I'll be your sun-and-moon shine
Just daily Bread.
I fear the small-b bread
(The kind that's oven-loved)
I won't have time to help Thee make
If from the house I'm shoved.

I know people do it (sigh)
Some are capable.
Some like automatons
Can help the load pull.

Like empty shells they clatter
From bare-clean homes to "Work".
It doesn't seem to matter
If intellect is shirked.

I think; therefore, I am.
If there's no time to think,
This "am" I am will die
At least perceptibly shrink.

<u>That's</u> the price that's <u>paid</u>
For increasing greenback cash.
Intuition slows down –
Preoccupied with dash –

Hither and yon
Helter and skelter
Up the down-staircase and through,
Physically fit
Mentally nit-wits
(I actually don't mean <u>you</u>.)

Proud individuals,
Together a mess,
A mosaic of colour and noise.
How will God understand
The courage beneath
'Less we take a moment to poise?

23.   December 1994

Astronomy

There is a powerful appeal
To preserving ancient tongues –
Sponged up so effortlessly
By the young.
Also there's the thought –
If they speak Chinese –
Maybe Earth won't get blown up –
O God, please …
But we've been taught so skillfully
That God equates with love –
That God really <u>has</u>
A Home for us Above …

Proxima Centauri
light-years away –
May have planets 'round it –
Who are we to say?

For th'uncharted path through space
They'll need a perfect map
Written in ONE language:
They'll need a trusty ship:
They'll need the food to get there,
And the courage to try,
The patience and the will
To NEVER say die.
Columbus never knew
He'd ever reach a shore.
We have to have the faith
Of those who've gone before –
Those in our history of <u>whatever</u> race
With the guts to look grim Death in the face,
And say …

O yes my life

Is very dear to me

But what is more important is human History.

The children of the future

Have to have a Home.

<u>That is the bottom line</u>.

So, as I end this poem,

Dear parents, give your children

Everything they <u>need</u>.

Most important, give them

GOOD BOOKS TO READ.

Not just words and pictures –

Facts and numbers too.

Like Star Gazers of old –

We're not yet through . . .

24.   1995

Eau, sacred eau

Worth more than any sou,

Each little drop

Is easier to digest

Than a coin stamped with a maple leaf

By our Imperial mint,

And is base of any man's largesse.

God keep this oh!

Glorious and clean.

Oh! Sacred eau

We need you squeaky clean.

Oh! Glorious eau

Make us all pristine.

Oh! Glorious eau

Of Universe the Queen.

25.   June 19, 1996

Do you want me, O God
To use a computer
Or to use a paintbrush instead?
How would Thou prefer that I use
All these bits and bites in my head?

To create works of beauty
Surely would be
A life-work worthy
For all to see,

Or to look at a screen
And try to master
A medium that says
"Faster! Faster!"

For my brain's stimulation
I would choose the mouse,
But for imagination,
For love of Creation,
I'd choose stagnation
And never leave the house.

I'd wield my brush
With all my force.
I'd ride my piano
Like a wild horse.

I'd sketch with hands so full of care
That each line would be a whisper there
Where Ecstasy came
And touched my Soul
While the paper recorded
A being Whole.

The following two poems were written while taking an Administrative Assistant course.

26. April 21, 1998

I took this course for something to do,
Something that would make cash.
Now I find a stalling in me,
A longing for something that lasts,
A career that will make a difference,
A profession to satisfy soul,
A desire to paint —
(Now isn't that quaint?)
In order to be whole.

27. February 25, 1998

Walking down these hallowed halls of learning
I find in me a simple kind of yearning
To be free, more alive,
To be willing to strive –
Face and conquer the day –
In my own nice way
A passion for freedom is burning.

28.

A Homemaker's Spring Song

As I sit sewing,
I feel a poem growing:
I feel a song coming on.
Soon grass will be growing,
Soon seeds will be sown,
Oh, Spring won't be so long!

It's Spring I await,
But in this tense state
There's someone else, it is true.
The day is long.
I save my song.
I wait, dear Love, for you.

The clock's steady tick
Is not very quick.
The hum of fridge fills the space.
There's a perfect whole.
There's integrity of soul
That time will ne'er erase.

Tomorrow's a day
I'll be looking for pay.
I won't be home near as much.
I won't have time
For making rhymes,
For Music, Art and such.

Before we say
Adieu to this day
Let's bring deserved tribute.
Its glow brings sheen
To everything
Gives wings to my soul's root.

29.   July 18, 1996

On the "Windows' Tutorial

Entering this pewter box
Is entering a different world –
A world peopled by
Others' imaginations.
Their industry, humour and understanding
Are evident
In their delightful and exciting creations.
Where will I go next?
I am humbled, yet emboldened, intrigued
By the step-by-step nature of learning.
These windows opening in front of me
Are like portholes,
Like camera lenses
Adjustable on command,
Surrounded by flapping, beckoning white sheers
That say, "Come. Enter"
And admit tantalizing summer breezes
Of a freshness that is as old
As Euclid.

30.

You can ………..
Row, row, row your boat
Gently down the stream.
You can ……….
Row, row, row your boat
As if life were a dream –
Or you can swim
With your fin
And a grin.
You can dive
And be really alive.
You can surprise

The ocean of eyes,
And disappear,
And again rise.
You can hide in the clear wet cool;
You can save yourself in the Pool.

31.   May 18, 1991

The solution to boredom is creativity.
This idea has had its nativity.
Let's hope I don't forget it.
Let's hope I live and sweat it,
And never again
Retreat into passivity.

32. November 2000

Gotta have my Goffee

This red tea
Is very tart --
Doesn't jump-start
My heart,
But makes a tart
And tangy
Engine of my tongue.

Better still
It gives me the impression
That I'm young.

In a dream
My Dad said
Sip this black.
Then you'll be able
To cook an egg.
It'll give you the strength.

I need the word "coffee'
To get out of bed
And I always will until I'm dead
The memory
Of that sacred scent
Is almost to me heaven-sent.

Some people drink coffee
All the day long,
Fill their bodies
With its dust.
For me, however,
Is it really a must?

To get up
In the morning
And keep on going
We need these memories
Of ashes glowing.

I know the fire
Is under my fingers
And on this monitor bright
But the familiar taste
Of carbon-black
Surely brings my memory back.

33.

This is a new day,
Brown and grey.
The houses are straight lines,
But higgledy-piggledy,
Clashing in colours
And built at different times.
The train is hooting
Its clarion call
To travel and action.

God, give me the will
To resist distraction!

34.

You've got to believe
That the earth is fertile.
You've got to cherish the sod.
Each moment spent in faith and hope
Brings you nearer God.

35.   September 15, 1998

I Sewed Him a Name-Tag

You try to be creative
And it just makes people mad.
You go a bit beyond the pale
And you just end up sad.

What can be learned from this
Is so hard to surmise.
I'm not sure this situation
Was made by God All-Wise.

Boys don't like mothers
Fooling with their clothes.
That's a truth
Everyone knows.

This truth extends to futures
When boys grow into men.
Just as they don't like sutures –
Don't go beyond a hem!

Don't monogram, or decorate,
Embroider or emboss,
For all the time you've dared to spend
Will be a total loss!

36.

Hair Loss

Thought I'd keep my hair
To express my rage
At the situation I'm in.
Then it was gone with a snip, snip, snip.
Now I have no lip, lip, lip,
And you can see my fleshy chin.

I can hope it'll grow again,
But at these many years old,
I fear that it will grow in <u>grey</u>.
Oh the winter! Oh the cold!
Oh the life lived without freedom!
Oh the naked and the dead!
O forgiveness for our sins!
May it grow in RED!

37.   September 30, 1996

Coffee

In my milky coffee
There's a shadow.
It's the same shadow
That exists at the heart of a flame.
It's a ghostly long-haired head
From Heaven and the past
And it says "You're not alone."

If I keep moving
From one milky café to the next,
All my life long, I'll survive.
I'll survive jealousy
With that strength inside me.
I'll survive all illness,
All depression, all loneliness,
And with the memory of the cross
Straightening my back,
I'll do it with my head high.

38. December 1997

Torture

My mind is not my friend sometimes.
It goes all amiss,
Worrying about the coffee.
Is it really this?
Is it really this, Lord
That is my decision?
Help me, Lord
To value my precision.
Help me to save money
Without compromising soul.
Make me awake;
Make me whole!

39.   November 11, 1996

No Fire Today

I wanted a fire –
To see the flames
Leap and cavort in the grate.
To burn the junk mail,
To feel the heat,
To give expression to hate.

I loved the fire;
I loved the beauty
The variations of red –
But today we remember.
We remember the war;
We exchange the flame with the dead.

They gave us a torch
To hold so high,
So high that we hold our breath.
We must not burn,
But only build
That life will endure after death.

Every particle of smoke
That invades the air
Means less O^2 to breathe.
The air we borrow
From grandchildren
Must satisfy <u>their</u> need.

The spitfire crashed;
The pilot died.
We mourn but quietly think –
Reserve our fuel for Andromeda
Lest civilization sink.

40. February 1, 2002

An Early Valentine – "The Kept Wife"

Gone, a chance –
I let it slip –
A chance to be like them,
Like those who slave for daily bread,
Whose sacrifice is hymn.

Who stand for hours
And handle cash
Amidst the hurly burly,
And let the world
The whole wide world
Know you are a girly.

Privileged,
I stand aloof,
Alone for most my time,
Active enough,
Yet not stressed-out,
Not worried about a dime.

And this I do,
Because of you,
Your unfailing support.
If you asked, "Do you love me?"
"'Deed I do!" I'd retort.

If you asked, "Do you need me?"
"'Deed I do!" I'd reply.
Without you, I'd be dismal,
Without you, I'd cry.
Without your cheerful grin,
My day wouldn't be complete.
I think you're great;
I think you're sweet;
I think you're really NEAT.

41.   February 8, 2000

Beginning

We do earnestly repent
And acknowledge our wrongs –
All the time we have cooked
Instead of writing songs.

All the T.V. we have watched
When Art could have been made,
All the arguments that resulted
Because prayers were not prayed.

We could not find the path.
It was hidden from our view.
We were leaping stone to stone
And missed quite a few.

Once Thou said, "Forgive them,
For they know not what they do."
Forgive <u>me</u> please, O Saviour,
For my contrition's true.

Let this music tell Thee
Of the love I feel.
Let each song give others
Contentment that is real.

42. September 17, 1996

O Dream that will not let me go
I put my hopeful trust in thee.
Continue in thy quest I will
'Though there's arthritis in my knee.

'Though there's arthritis in my hip
I won't leave that sinking ship.
Even if lumbago takes my <u>arm</u>
Still I'll strive to be school marm.

Oh God, Thou gave me many a chance
But I was too proud to dance.
I didn't know today I'd feel
That those teenage dreams were real.

I followed the urge to be a mother
As if there were no other
Life work that I wished to do
In this human zoo.

But I don't regret that I gave
My three fine sons
(Who all behaved)
My years that were young.

It's now that in these fading years
When hubby's finished all his work
That my body gives me cause for tears
As well, holidays tempt me to shirk.

God will work a miracle
Send me to school
So I can exonerate
The Golden rule.

In this hope
I will do my best
Bend to the plowshare –
Ace the test –
Launder the sheets – Bake the pies –
And collect the kisses for my prize.
But I won't forget our plan

And, as an office drudge,
Or while washing dishes
Or while making fudge,
I'll dream of little children
And teaching them to read,
Because Thou and I know
'Tis me they need.

43. September 17, 1996

God! Why inflame me with desire
To ignite the living brain cells
With hope and life and thought
And make the little children
Love the Earth your hands have wrought.
O, give some kind of sense
In all this despair
That something, somewhere is good and fair.

Save that one recalcitrant limb
My body sings a healthy hymn.
I am infected with a desire to teach.
Is that goal impossible to reach?

The classroom situation
Where they run around all day
Is one where in pain I'd dearly have to pay.

I don't want to be in pain.
You have already paid that price
And given me the freedom
To about sacrifice think twice.

Teaching is creative and challenging and hard,
A career all-consuming for those so starred.

My first career is mother.
Other things take second place.
My family has to come first.
This I have to face.

I chose to have three children
And doing so, denied
The world a clever teacher
And myself true peace inside.

In study and in learning
We find profound joy.
In sharing insights, reasons,
Find hope, both girl and boy.

I have been given gifts
Of body and of mind.
I know that I must share them
In my earthly time.

If all I have is Pen
And creative thought
Then may that be enough for me
And may the kids be taught!

(In the year 2005
I'll decide if I would survive
Adventure in a classroom.)
Meanwhile I'll forget my dream
And try not to scream
As I wield the broom.
I'll hang on real tight
And try to write
Stories, songs and poetry
That approach sublimity,
Show creativity,
And inspire the young tremendously.

44. Sept. 28, 1996

Oh Lord, Thou art too far away.
Thou'rt like a star on high –
And so I'll give to little plants
A watchful eye.
They'll give to me
Some tasty strength,
And help me go
The hero's length –
The extra row.

45. July 28, 1996

God has been with me
These few days
As I've thought it over –
How best to end our days
Knee-deep in clover.
What has been given me
By my better half
Is a careful study
Of a sensible path.

If only I could forget
The days of my youth
And that spicy French teacher
Who spoke the truth –
That beautiful receptionist
I also recall
But her job – not as brainy, at all.

Today's secretary's jobs
Are harder, I know
More challenging too,
And you can't be slow.

But that cheerful school teacher
Whom I'll never forget
Makes me envy teachers yet.

46.

Morning Visions

Four V's of long-necked geese I saw
Honking their way North,
In military precision,
Sunlit bellies agleam.

Then two large black ravens
Gracefully flew across my path.
Then a sunkist robin
Caroled my welcome home
From the top of our highest tree.

47.   July 19, 1996

Morning has come,
And with it the knowledge
That I must create.
With one's own happiness
One combats hate.

Today when I got up
I had to wait and wait
To get to my paintbrush –
And then it was too late.
Better rush
And write a poem
To sate my worried pate.

48. July 17, 1996

Last night I dreamt I was true to You
Even unto death.
How wonderful to be true to You
Even to my last breath.
I was totally given to the service of Good
And always did just what I should.
I was absorbed in giving Love
And felt a connection to Above.
Would that this would all come true
And I be ever true to You.

49.

"There will be a job for me
Somewhere down the way."
This my song of faith and hope
Comforts me today.

There will be a boss for me
Other than my mate,
Other than the One above
Who says, "Don't get up late."

50.   October 26, 1997

Fowl Supper

What a bright bubbly
Burst of people
All a-munchin' there.
I had to squirm –
There wasn't room
To squeeze into my chair!

51.   May 5, 1996

Freeze Frame #1

Crickets chirping, ducks quacking,
Sunset reflected in the flooded marsh,
Balmy air belying
The winter that's been harsh;
Bike kindly gripping
As it takes me on my way –
Thanks for the beauty of this
Spring day!

52.

The rays of the sun say "Run."
The giant gold orb says "Scurry."
The brilliant appeal
Makes me feel
Like it's saying
"Why don't you <u>hurry</u>?"

But it's Sunday
(I say in reply)
What work is right to do?
Is writing right?
Is singing right?
(As Father wished me to?)

<u>Tomorrow</u> is the Runday.
Today is named for <u>you</u>,
And for the Son, spelled with an "o",
Whose history we have learned to show
In faithful word and pantomime
Every week at this time.

That is the work I'll do today —
So, glorious sun in your array,
Glistening beads on diamond snow —
Listen, for e'en when you're away
Trillions of years from today
They'll still be singing hymns, I pray.

53.   December 10, 1998

Where is God in All This?

I feel as blue as the clouds that enfold the sunset yonder,
A moody blue, part grey, that tests my will to live.
What would Christ think of the
giddiness of Christmas, I ponder.
Would His answer be, "Live and let live?"

Or does it grieve Him as it does me,
The division that exists
Between CHRIST-mass as it should be
And the broken Xmas that it is.

The famous prayer He said to pray
Taught in school no longer,
What would He think of that, I ponder.
Junior Choir a memory,
Faint, distant, sweet,
Youngsters far more concerned with what they get to eat,
Four-letter words known and said by youth universal,
Rap and heavy-metal singers shout
and scream and hurtle....

Oh yes, life is wonderful –
We can talk to Timbuctoo –
We can add to sixty zillion –
We have everything in zoos ….

But there are species vanishing,
The world is getting hot,
And does what we say mean anything?
Often – not a lot.

54.

He didn't even notice
And I had some great clothes on.
Why, why do I try?

He didn't even notice
And I had my good hose on,
But I'm not going to cry.

I still have the pride
And the self-satisfaction
From knowing I looked my best,
That will help me get tonight
A well-earned hearty <u>rest</u>.

55.   May 6, 1995

This Music thing
Seems to be a strain
But how can I let it
Go down the drain?

Thought my fingers were too smart
To tap a copied beat
But now melodic notes
Seem the wrong sort of sweet.

Is Nero fiddling
Throughout my labored heart?
Will Rome burn
If this career I start?

I do not live by bread alone.
I need the cheerful sound
Of humans to somewhat degree –
But is this solid ground?

Cooking is the strong art
And cutting settles rage.
This is the truth that will carry Man
From age to brand new Age.

56.

Ode to the Cow

O Beast that graces oft our table,
Child of she who mooed beside the Stable,
Who has roamed the Earth as long as Man has –

We love to eat you.
Your taste is incomparable.
You eat things that must taste like Hell.

You can produce a horrible smell.
You have very little between your ears,
And yet you almost reduce me to tears.

The generosity of your constant gift
Gives me an unsurpassable lift.
Smarter than many human mothers,
You give the gift of your relaxed udder.
With no discrimination
You give to every nation.
(Of course you have to have the money.
Then it sort of isn't funny.)

But YOU demand no fee-
Only grass and hay to see
Only time to chew your cud –
For that you donate precious blood.

You don't know your life will end
When the axe strikes,
'Cause your brain hasn't 'nuff
Bits and bites.
The Lord made you slow of brain,
Slow of speed,
Like a dinosaur who never learned
How to read.
Therefore you've been chosen
To be eaten,
Fried into Chinese dinners –
Made into sandwiches that are winners.

Land that you occupy
That is not arable –
(This is the part
that is unbearable) –
Land that could hold
Factories and homes
Is where you are allowed to roam.

What about folks that'd love
To build a shack
And share a little space,
Who'd love to get out
Of their urban rat-race,
Who'd like to immigrate from the country they're in
And ask Mrs. Cow to moooove over and
Let their children in?

The brains of these kids
Need Prairie space
To grow to inspire
Our human race.

Let's improve
Our human crowd
And not by giant Mammon
Be cowed.
Let's grow children
In the space
And gradually
Gluttony
Erase.

57.   July 3, 2000

Safe Landing

(On leaving a secretarial position at the United Church and joining the Anglican Church of the Messiah, and building a garden for them.)

Left the United Church
In a search
Full of doubt,
For some clout,
Searching for an answer,
I was an antsy dancer;
I couldn't settle down and type

Mistrusting the tune I had to pipe,
Looking for More than what was offered,
Spurning the justice that was proffered,
Spurning the wage
Turning the page
Moving on, spurning the song,
Seeking the Spirit I felt in my youth
Spirit of Answer
Spirit of Truth.

I found a Christ
Streaming with fruit
Beyond the pale of the birthday suit.
I envisioned a Garden
Of flowers for Him
A grateful 'Thank Thee' for forgiveness of sin.
That garden holds herbs
But none will there be
That do not encourage sobriety;
And I've found a Church
That satisfies need,
That provides comfort; thus, the Garden's seed.

Prayer for the Junior Choir

Peace!

Peace!

Clean breath!

Keep us from death!

Let our souls soar aloft

When we die.

Let our souls soar aloft

While we live,

Sometimes –

Just enough to help us hope.

Keep us from smoke. Keep us from dope.

Let us forget the *ennui*

And remember that

Our country's free!

Let the songs that we shall sing

Express our love – and everything!

59.   February 24, 1994

Naïve?

If all the children could be weaned
From the electronic screens,
If they could stop being passive and start
Learning a tongue different from their own
What a difference it would make in their hearts!
How they'd stop being glued
To the soap-opera style
Of the omnipresent tube!
How they'd stop being enthralled
With the guns!
How they'd lose fascination
With sexual gyration
And start finding that
<u>Thinking</u>'s fun.
How they'd become aware
That in Canada there's a <u>pair</u>
Of complicated languages at least.
How they'd learn
That mankind has come very, very far

From being a beast.
How they'll learn respect
For our neighbour Quebec
And open eyes to the cultures all o'er.
How they'll find ideas
That are worthwhile repeating
And maybe lose interest in war.

60.

6:40 a.m.

Cloud cover
Lying with a smoky scalloped
Edge
Contrasting the low luminescence.

Lady Moon beckoned
Dimly half-visible,
Veiled –
Now she's gone.

61.   April 13, 2000

The wind is like a furbelow
Pushing from behind,
Created in an icy furnace
To torment humankind.
The sun shines benignly,
But too remote to heat,
Although it brings
Sure hope of Spring –
Oh, won't that be a treat!

62. June 25, 2000

Halcrow Marsh

The marsh is alive with the sound of beings –
Crickets, songbirds of various types,
Alive with the sight of green upon green –
One of my favourite sights,
Alive with a breeze of refreshing air
In which the soul delights.
<u>Here</u> is the balm
For the daily *lutte*.
<u>Here</u> is a promise
For a restful night.

63. May 22, 1992

Chez moi

I have a magic machine.
It fractures carrot into smithereens.
It massacres cabbage greens.
It sounds like a screaming
Automatic gun –
But when it's done …
When it's done …
I look in wonder and in awe
At ….VOILA! ….<u>COLESLAW</u>!

64.

If there were a Planet
Anywhere in the sky
Anywhere humans could live
Somewhere we could fly,,,
Then I would spend
Every charitable cent
On sending people there –
I would help found a colony
No matter where …
But even with our keenest eyes
We can't see such a star …
If we accept reality …
We really <u>can't</u> go far.
Physically we're stuck on Earth
How can we cope with that?
By concentrating on improving
Our multilingual <u>chat</u> …
<u>That</u>'s how to find true Peace on Earth
And mutual understanding.
<u>That</u>'s how we'll make our personal
Moon landings.

It doesn't take a lot of dough
Or technological know-how;
All it takes is over and over

To say "vache means cow".
Once you have absorbed
Another's way of speech
Understanding a new culture
Is well within reach;
So keep plugging at whatever
Language you are learning
And together we will keep
The lamp of Hope burning …
Until the astronauts say
"Yes, we have a landing."

65.

Pray a reverent prayer on Christmas Eve
That escapes the Universe.
May hope and strength then follow –
You know things could be worse!
After death we'll all
Be in shining Light!
Dwell in Love and Peace –
Justice is our fight!

66.   December 5, 2000

We have a private bedroom
In which hangs a cross.
In this room we ponder
Just who is the boss.
I say that it is Jesus.
He says it is the Free.
- We're both right -
And Truth is dripping from the tree
In sap of neon honey
And maple syrup molasses.
It intones the dong
Of the truth that lasses and lasses –
"His service is perfect Freedom."

67.

How can I express
This "great"-ful moment?
Depress the whiteness of this page
With ink of such rainbow hue
That will convey my gratitude?
Impress the reader with my joy?
Repress all angst for ever
And ever?
I'll say

                              Amen.

68. 1969

A poem for you,
If you like poems
And can read
Then glue your eyes on this.
Heed.

Bullets will ne'er succeed.
They're only rocks
And rocks are meant
For scrambling on
And filling up kid's socks.

So let's build a mountain of garbage like that
And when it's climbed
Stick on the top a mad hat.
In the winter we can ski on it.
In the summer we can lie
And bask in the sun
Or swim if water is nearby.

And best of all
All those guys
That have been taught else
Will have less to fool around with
That makes them remember war.
I didn't rhyme.
Did I still score?

69.

In fourteen hundred and ninety-two
Columbus sailed the ocean blue;
In nineteen hundred and ninety-two
There's hope for me: there's hope for you.
The peace pipe blows soap bubbles;
The answer is Clean Air.
The flag is a sheet of Blank Paper
Unspoiled and fair.
The hope is in Control
Over needle, knife, and pen
That artists share the love
– And absorb the pain –

70.   September 30, 1995

Autumn Song

The din of lawnmowers fills the air.
I comb the grass as if it were hair.
I comb the grass with my rake.
What'll I bake? What'll I bake?

71.   May 14, 1995

Thank Thee for my body;
Please be in my soul;
Keep us sane and strong and true
To Thee, o perfect Whole.

72.   December 20, 1995

The gift of meat, my Lord
Is more that I can bear.
I know that I must eat it
Just as I breathe air.

Its taste is so delicious;
It gives me strength to move.
To do without would be
An act of sacrificial love.

To be honest, I like it.
It's wonderful to me.
It helps me do the things I do;
It helps me see.

Teach me how to do without
Those sugary treats
Rather than the vital good,
And strengthening meat.

73.

God was the Word;
The Bible was writ
And, billions of words later on,
There's a monitor here as we sit
Still trying to write a song,
Still trying to fathom
The depth of a love
That gave us a bountiful Earth,
Now grimly come to terms with the fact
That of room there is a dearth,
That somehow we have to find the gas
To propel us into space,
Where there'll be room
To colonize
And spread the human race.
For now it's only robots
That can "man" a star-bound ship.
They have only started
To make the needed trip.

74. July 28, 1996

Secretary or French Teacher?

God has been with me
These few days
As I've thought it over
How best to end my days
Knee-deep in clover.
Sure what has been given me
By my better half
Is a careful, steady, study
Of a sensible path.
If only I could forget
The days of my youth
And that spicy French teacher
Who spoke the truth,
That beautiful receptionist
I also recall
But her job didn't take
As many brains at all.
Today secretary's jobs
Are harder I know

More challenging too
And you can't be slow,
But that cheerful school teacher
I'll never forget
Makes me envy
Teachers yet.

75.

Dear God, I thank you for my life.
I thank You that I am a wife
I thank You that I am a mother,.
That I have a sister, that I have brothers,
That we still have a mother
Of whose like there is no other.
Help me live 'til 2050.

Keep it happy! Keep it nifty!
Help me use my gifts as You see fit
That I don't make a mess of It.
Now I'm going in the right direction
Let me know if I need correction

Thank You for listening to my prayer:
Thank you for breath; thank you for air
And because You're sort of out of reach (sometimes)
Thank You for the gift of speech.

76. June 17, 2002

I've just got up; dawn's grey light is near.
Before I dance the hymn that I hold dear
May God allow my first impressions here.

It's Monday and we've had our celebration;
We've spoken of our God-inspired elation;
We've told Him of our hungers and frustration,
And now it's time for this week's tribulation.

But in this land so full of milk and honey
We must beware the call of too much money;
We must be mindful of our other need
And not allow predominance of greed.

We must beware temptations to be lazy;
We must keep balance so we don't go crazy;
We must focus on what we have to eat,
Be grateful for the bitter <u>and</u> the sweet.

Outside beckons fresh balmy air
The sky has turned blue and white and fair.
The lawn and flowers show a gardener's care.
I'll go and dance the Morning Lord's Prayer.

77.

3 January, 2000 A.D.

Christ was born at Noel this year.
I'm not sure where or how
But people weren't really swearing
When they whispered, "Holy Cow!"

It was more a word of reverence
A sign of awed delight
As the 2000 corner's turned
We're hoping the ship's <u>tight</u>.

We're hoping that we're all tuned in
To the Compassion Channel:
Curiosity ain't enough
(Even if it <u>is</u> red flannel!)

We need to love our neighbours
And feel that love returned –
'Though 'tis a global village
Dignity must be given, not earned,

And the Holy Cow's a space ship.
We all hope it will fly,
And that the astronauts have a safe trip
And lots of apple pie.

78.

Holy Communion in the United Church of Canada

… And when the sheet was lifted
There under was round Bread
And sterling goblet Cup.
Again he is not dead.

Once more my heart has risen
Responding to such proof.
Not only in the sky dwells God
But under human roof.

79.   January 8, 1996

Each brain is a garden
And in it are some rocks –
Places that one will not change –
Hardened spots.

For some the Bible's words
Are objects without life –
Eternal lumps that cannot change
Or be tampered with.

Every word in that Book (they claim)
Must be swallowed whole
Hook, line and sinker
If Truth is to be told.

I rather think of humankind
As a river
And the Bible as the Spring
Which ran into a torrent of Science
Ding dong Splash dong ding.

Now the two are intertwined
And dependent on each other –
Science the logical Father
Religion the loving Mother.

These two gods will guide us
If we cherish both
With numbers and with letters
Communication will be Truth.

Your ABC's are just as great
As 1, 2, 3, 4, 5.
Man needs more than dollars and bread
To keep alive.

So stick with the Christian Church
Don't fear being "strange".
It is tied to humanity's past
But it is the church of change.

80.

He, She or Thee
Who knows what are Thou?
If Jesus was Thy Son,
In truth Thou art a He
For Jesus called Thee Father
And He wouldn't lie.

No, Christ was not a liar;
He was too good for that.
His history of rising again
Must have been a fact.
Others have said that it happened so.
If this is really true
And God is personal!
If God really listens
To our earnest prayers
We should pray a little every day –
Real, earnest prayers,
As we mount the heavenly stairs.

81.

Who can comprehend little boys
Who like and adore war toys?
Why do they think it is fun
To pretend to kill with a gun?

The skill of aiming
I can understand
Is invaluable for those
Who live on the land.
The basic drive
To hunt for meat
Gives us sustenance to eat.
But why do little boys roar:
"Let's play WAR!"

82.   February 24, 1997

We are not afraid.
We are traveling to the light.
From the light of our beginning
To the light of that Shining Way
We huff and puff the coffee chant
That gets us through the day.
We think we can
And think we can
Until we knew we could.
We move
With quietness and speed
As we knew we should,
And our reward
Is just to know that,
Really, we've been "good".

With our mouths set on "smile"
And our heads held high,
We shall swim
We shall walk
We shall fly.

With our mouths set so firm

That no air can escape

We dream of the swim

We shall have in a lake.

With our moths "prêt" to laugh

And our thoughts in control

We contemplate

The Perfect Whole.

Around us the din and the hubbub may reign

But inside, all is peace, all is health, all is sane…

83. July 26, 1996

In the morning
When one wakes up
After a dutiful prayer
There is water
There is light
There is air.

And in these times so advanced
One can compute
So much to be thankful for
That you can't refute.

Why dream for rainbows in the sky
Under other suns?
Why hope for costly changes
That might not e'en be fun?

Why should I long for schools
When office life
Might be perfect
For this wife?

"Minor degenerative changes"
In this leg of mine
Decree that I find a job
Where sitting will be fine.

The cross I bear
Of a vanished dream
Will not make me
Curse or scream.

The children of the future
Are all my hope and aim
Preserving Mother Earth for them
Is an important game.

More vital than cards
Or golf
Is the vanquishing
Of self.

To leave for the kids
This waaater, this air
To slow down pollution
Everywhere.

To be more like my mother
Is a goal I will pursue
And time spent vainly chasing the past
Is time that I might rue.

84. April 3, 1998

Everything's revealed again –
The sun's rays pick up
Las year's pop cans, and the dead brown grass
Highlighted by slivers of ice or snow.
The car's windows are all frosty;
There's ice upon the marsh,
But the lilting of the birds
Promise a day not too harsh.

85.

I say to the blue,
"Oh, Blue, how are you?'
I say to the gold,
"Sun, are you old?'

The sun says,
"Yes, I am old,
But oh, I do shine,
And so must you —
Yes, all of the time."

86.

On Thanksgiving

The ground is brown; the trees are black;
The sky is mottled grey.
Summer is over and winter is near
On this Thanksgiving Day.

The air is making my face stiff;
It's lost its summer balm.
My hands are rolled inside my gloves
Into a fist to keep them warm.

The boxcars wait, mute and still
For an impulse from the engine
While the trees think of Spring
Whose impulse comes from heaven.

87.   July 1, 2001

The sky is cerulean blue,
The sun a dazzling gold —
Is it really true
That I am growing old?

On such a day it matters not
The age one has achieved —
On such a day as this, you see,
God satisfies <u>all</u> need.

88. April 30, 2000

The colours are not harsh
O'er this sunseted marsh,
They glow ethereally –
An amber kind of rose
Diffuses into blue
And touches me–
Deeply, calmly.
A pink cloud or two
Slices through the blue
All below is black and tan.
The serenity in this evening view
Speaks of a century's span.

89.   Late winter 2001

The wind sighs,"No!",
Whistles through each branch
Effecting primordial dance.
Shell pink meets blue
In roseate dawn.
And me?
My fur's still on.
The skies as well are clad in fluff,
And for me that's good enough.

90.   April 28, 2000

It's wonderful!
Spring is happening
Again this year.
And all I can think about
Is coffee, wine, and beer.
They seem to be needed now
To have a fulfilled life.
They seem to be making me
A better wife.
The only thing the matter
Is the problem with my bladder.
(Don't talk of that in public now, my dear!)
You know what I think:
I'll continue to drink
And step up the exercise all year!

91.

Prayer for the Life of my Seeds

I will shush my voice 'til Sunday,
And not say Thy glorious Name
'Til it's said with such devotion
    All swearing is in vain.

I will spend my days in labour
    And refrain from idle chat;
I will try to be pristine and pure
    And regal like my cat.

I will bend my knees to Thee
Each morning and each night ---
    If only, O Creator ----
Give me, of seedlings, SIGHT.

92.   February 21, 2002

It's that wonderful, tremulous time
When winter sunlight glows
With a new ethereal shine
That speaks of Springtime shows.

A November Poem

The view is all in brown lines;
Grey is the sky.
On such a day as this
Men did die.
They gave up their lives
For the freedom that we share.
Is there any one of <u>us</u>
Who would take such a dare?

Canada is Happy Land
Here there is fast food.
Here the traffic's not too bad
And the air is good.
But if the war had been lost,
If Hitler had his way,
Even on the sunny days
Our sky would now be grey.

94.   December 18, 2001

> The sky is too blue, the sun too bright
> For complaints today.
> The snow is such a brilliant sight
> It takes all my blues away.

95.   April 30, 2002

Start your day with a pencil
And your happiness is sure.
Start your day with a pencil
And your serenity is pure.
Some start their day with toothbrush;
Some reach for brush for hair.
For me, the tool conveying light
Is beyond compare.

96. February 3, 2002

'Though on the one hand I love you
On the other I am furious
You deprived me of opportunity
To be curious.

I should be thankful, yes, I know,
For the freedom that I have –
Freedom granted by your work
So that I don't have to slave.

I swear that I'll use this freedom
In constructive ways.
Darn it all, I'll <u>get</u> a job –
A job that really <u>pays</u>.

There are more things in life, I know
Than money and than work.
There's art and music, reading too –
All those things that I do
When laziness doesn't lurk.

But a <u>purpose</u> for life must be found –
A <u>reason</u> for one's life –
And darn it, it <u>isn't</u> enough
Just to be a wife.

Because I'm <u>your</u> wife, yes, it's good;
Life is interesting;
Your conversation's smart,
And you are fascinating.

But I'm a person too
Who has ever-present needs
And one which drives me now
Is a need to succeed.

I know that I failed
That I shied at the kick-off,
That I nervously gave up
That I coughed at lift-off …

Only God can forgive me.
Only God can help me now.
He's my e'er-present Friend
And He will show me how –

How to get back on track
To somehow go on living
To be happy, not sad
To be good and keep on giving.

97.

It's a Miracle

I see today the ducks returned.
They found a welcome here
In the water of this marsh.
They're twittering and honking now
Of a land that's not too harsh.
On the puddly grassy flat
I see dots of black and white –
The seagulls and the ducks are sharing –

Some in flappy flight.
There is a chill in the spring air;
Flecks of snow are swooping down
But I have seen a miracle;
The ducks are back in town.

98.

Oh God
I've lost my diary today
And I don't know how to draw.
I lay in bed too long.
I put food in my maw.
Yet Thou art all-forgiving still –
Because of Thy holy will
There is a place here full of birds,
A place where there are no words,
A place of gulls and ducks and geese,
A place of beauty and of peace.

99.   May 8, 2002

My love affair with the pencil and pen
Lasted thirty years too long;
These toys that pleased a teenage girl
Are, for a woman, wrong.
A mother's tools are pots and pans,
Needles, threads and cloth,
Broom and dustpan, rake and hoe,
The Bible's words against sloth.
Today computers also are a tool which she must use,
And books, so that her mind she doesn't lose.

100.

I must take in words
For mental food
Each and every day –
Sit and read and study
Part of my time away.
This is the rest,
The mental rest
All human brains require,
So that we may go on and on
And never tire.

101.

God uses His agent, the Sun,
To bring light and hope to the world.
We notice it 'specially in Spring
When the beauty is unfurled;
But he used his only Son
To do likewise long ago,
To reveal His love
In an undying way
That must be treasured evermore.

102.   October 29, 2002

Raisins and almonds are food for the Jew;
Christians love Bread and Wine,
But those who worship the blue dome above –
For them is there still time?
The constellations can't be Friends
They are composed of stars;
Stars are great big masses
Of chemicals and dust
That give off Light,
And light is God.

So maybe they *are* Friends –
Like the flashlight and the candle –
Trusty stevedores
That help us get a handle.
There is one constellation
That is shaped like a man
In the eyes of the beholding
Astronomers of yore.
Once there was a Man
Who became our Christ

Symbolized by Wine, the preserved grape.
Grapes don't grow in Manitoba;
Cranberries do.
Local food is cheapest
Even in a zoo.
Drying is preserving;
So is fermentation;
Drying doesn't give you
The same elation.
So we must never lose
The power of the wine;
It is always Jesus
Throughout endless time,
But wine is expensive,
That we all know,
And yet we need Forgiving Love,
Everywhere we go.
So, as you live life's journey,
Take Jesus with you.
Read a little Bible every night,
Say His prayer every day
BEFORE your daily bread.
Join the joyful tribe once a week,
I know you listen when He speaks.
Think of His great courage

As you swallow each cranberry.
One each day
Reminds me of His Blood.

'Twas shed because He loves us.

Orion in the sky
Was also originated
By the hand of God.
The shape of a hunter –
Or the shape of a Man?
Once pinned on a cross, now free
Defiantly glorious
Starlit and beckoning, saying,
"Sinner, lovest thou ME?"

103.   November 26, 2002

A Grace Before Dinner

Dear Lord,
    May this meal suit us down to our toe,
    May it be not too fast, not too slow –
    The conversation interesting, the music low –
    May the candle gleam brightly
    On the newly-shined table,
    And may the food make us
    Quick, compassionate, and able.

                              Amen

104.　　　　　　　　　　　　　　　　February 7, 2002

Before it was so clear
Between you and I, my dear.
I cooked; you brought in *l'argent*.
Now, *tout est différent*.

The reason I applied for a job
Is that I was afraid of death —
Of not giving the world the best
Of my ability,
Of "retiring" too early.

Now a menace has entered our home.

A dissatisfaction —
Staying at home
No longer has
The same attraction.

I was truly happy here
Earlier this winter –
'Til I started worrying.
Boy, what a sinner!

I pray that God
May give me grace
To be happy again,
And to
"This woman's place
Is in the home"
Say, "Amen".

105. November 9, 2002

I'm married to a man both gentle and strong.
The summers are short; the winters are long.
Yet in our hearts we keep a song –
It varies from day to day.
The tuneless whistle that carries him through
The dishes and all of that truck
Is a sound that is all mixed up with his breath.
Separate them? Good luck!
But his eyes have the keen alertness
I saw on Day #1;
'Tho thirty-three years have come and gone
He still believes in fun.

106.   January 11, 2003

I know that I'm not stupid,
And I know that I'm not crazy.
I'm not extremely pretty,
And I'm not extremely lazy.
I'm just a human being,
And sometimes life is mazy.
Sometimes folks are cruel;
Sometimes skies are hazy.

But the sunshine is grey matter
Which operates just fine.
I try to have faith, hope and love;
I try to walk the line.
Cruelty I just forget;
Dark nights have stars remembered.
Never has despair
Really meant hope sundered.

107.   March 12, 2006

(a comment on the rapidly-increasing secular condition of our society)

Here's to the kids
That perform on the ice —
The kids that fight for the puck,
The kids that stretch
Eyes, hands and hearts,
And believe, dear God, just in <u>Luck</u>!

108.

(This poem was written for one of my sons, and accompanied a gift of painting materials.)

Untitled — Undated Therefore Timeless? Therefore Meaningless?

Your great-grandfather's name was Art;
Your grandfather was inspired;
Through me you have received the gift
Of unquenchable fire.

The day of birth you got it;
It is yours for life eternal;
These paints are only tools
To channel it — explore
With colour further, further
Than the <u>outside</u> of your skull –
To go inward more and more
And give the world your all.

These tools are your freedom
From everything in life –
All stress and pain can vanish –
Treat the brush as a wife –
Paint whatever you wish,
E. g. an idea or a fish –

If it clicks in your brain,
Let <u>us</u> share the pain,
And the ecstasy of birth.
Leave some of You on Planet Earth!

109.　　　　　　　　　　　　　January 15, 2000

There is something about today ...

Maybe it is the dove-like grey ...

Maybe it is the silver-lined clouds ...

Maybe it's the white blanket of snow,
Or the honest humble brown of the
wintering-over vegetation ...

Maybe it is the discreet silence
Of the row of modest dwellings,

Or the distant shouts of children at recess

Or the hum of distant traffic

Or the twittering conversation of the birds,

Whatever it is,
Something today speaks of
Peace.

110. August 11, 1994

What you see is what you see
Always has been and will be
Why should one assume that
What you <u>see</u> is what you <u>get</u>?

Little things impinge on eyes
Could bring pleasure, I surmise.
Why isn't that enough?
Why must we be so TOUGH?

Little children coming near
Lovely *objets d'art*
Are taught, "Don't touch."
If you want to be smart."

Adults too, of today
Have to learn how to say
Inside their skulls – "Wait a sec!
Liberties should not be taken.
Our self-control must re-awaken!"

111. March 6, 2006

O woodpecker,
Dining there,
Beating the bugs
Out of that dead tree –
Won't you let me past?

At last
You've stopped pecking,
And found a meal.
This is real
Nature at work.

Morning Coffee

The pow'r of the sun
Requires a response
Equal in intensity and shine.

Oh moon-glow
Dead-mouse
Cream
Connect me to a dream.
Connect me to my Sunday wine.

Oh, sore-eyes,
Back to bed
Try to join the living dead.
Or is it the dead-alive?
Better still – I'll bake bread
Into this new day I'll dive.

113.   June 15, 2002

Sing to the Lord a New Song

This is a new song,
But it has an old theme.
It's about a miracle,
A come-true dream.

It's about health
And joy and love
That I have received
Because God
Perceived my need.

I can't explain it anyhow.
It's more than my studies –
More than my Yoga
Or herbal teas –
It's more than getting a good night's sleep
Eating well and exercise
Although these all play a part –
It's Jesus' blood and sacrifice.

Just as in the old days
When He cured the lame
Jesus did for me
The very same.

I owe it to my Lord
This health that I feel
This joy every morning
This sanity that's real.

My song was a painting, Lord,
Now it must be new
So I'll study stars instead
In honour of You.

114. March 16, 1991

Hurrah for Herb Teas!

Hurray for Herb Teas!
Some are gentle, some suggest spice;
Most are very, very nice –
So hot and clear and honest –
With honey they are sweet.
They give you warmth and taste and goodness
And, as well, a good night's sleep!

115. February 12, 1991

Wake up, my eyes —
No drugs, no caffeine.
Wake up, my eyes;
It's time to be seen.

It's time to see —
More important still.
Wake up, my eyes.
It's an effort of will.

116. April 15, 1992

The god of garbage looks askance;
He sees what is thrown out;
He shakes His head in wonder;
He goes into a pout.

Things He sees like plastic pails, dishrags, towels clothes
Broken things that still have parts –
Others could use those.
Piles of multi-shaped debris
Rising to the sky
He thinks of use that could be made
And lifts His shoulders – why?

117.

Humble, pastel, faded napkins
Faded, aged, yet strong.
There is strength in those woven fibres –
You've lasted ten years long!

Your colour's not as vibrant
As 'twas in your youth,
But the paper garbage you've saved the world
Is your redeeming truth.

118. October 16, 1991

It's a good day.
The ground is covered with frozen water
interspersed with puddles,
But the main road is bare.
The grass is cloaked in glass
But balmy is the air.
The sun is escaping from dark pillows
In a golden shimmer
And the sky is a wondrous combination
Of blue and grey and white.
It's time for dinner!

119.   October 28, 1992

Slam goes the door
And all of a sudden
The house is deathly quiet.
The air is ominously still.
Empty, waiting.
Time hangs omnipotent and inscrutable
As the new Boss;
And I turn
Longing for a prayer
With strength enough
For this Day.
Keep me sane.
Alleluia, Praise the Lord, Life is great.
Amen.

120.

Christ died that we might live.
That's the thought that keeps me going.
That's the thought that keeps me sewing.

That's the hope I aim to feel—
And yet, it isn't really real.
It's a hope shrouded in mystery.
It's a hope relying on history.

We <u>do</u> need the Lord's Prayer
To keep things in perspective.
We need a Being that can hear us
When we're introspective.
But please, Lord, don't come back.
I don't want a virgin birth.
I don't think that is what will
Save the Earth.

<u>We</u> must work so that <u>He</u> doesn't have to.
<u>We</u> must let Him lie in Peace.
We must find the goals to live for –
The <u>concrete</u> goals that we can reach.

Mars is the red Planet in the sky.
We have the technology; it's the next frontier.
Why not send our brightest and best
Up there the next available year?

We need to learn why the rivers dried up –
Why Mars never greened at all.
We should go and *terraform* it,
Make it a habitable ball.

What else should humanity strive for?
Where else is there to go?
There's killing each other; there's feeding each other.
Please tell me; I'd like to know.

If you have suggestion better than this
To Man's aggressive drive,
Please tell me and we'll share a fish
And maybe both survive.

What lies ahead no one can tell.
It's the result of what we plan for.
It's what the good guys want
And what the leaders pray for.

Let's say a prayer for Astronauts!
Let's put our money on courage!
Let's keep humanity on the top shelf
And take wonder out of storage!

121.   May 24, 1992

O
Thou who lives beyond the sun —
Help me throughout the daily run;
Be with me and do not part;
Be in my soul and in my heart.

122.   January 3, 1990

Inspiration from Somewhere on a Sleepless Night

Chasing a molecule through the nebula,
Hoping to find it …
Hoping to find it …
Chasing a molecule through the nebula –
There!

123.

Ideas are so wonderful –
They keep me from being bored.
Without ideas I know
My mind would be a morgue!

First you take a theory;
Then you deduce,
Just like taking an orange
And from it making juice.

But then I start to play around
With lime and lemon too –
The ideas I've invented
Are the thoughts that make me <u>me</u>!
The ideas you've invented
Are the thoughts that make you <u>you</u>!

124. December 21. 1991

He, She or Thee
Who knows what are Thou.
If Jesus was Thy son
In truth Thou art He,
For Jesus called Thee Father
And He wouldn't lie.
It doesn't matter,
But it would be nice to know
Before I die.
Yes, Christ was not a liar.
He was too good for that,
So the tale about rising again
Must have been a fact.
Others also said
That it happened so.
If this is true
And God is really Personal!
If God really listens

To our earnest prayers!
Then we should pray a little every day –
Real earnest prayers –
As we mount
The heavenly stairs...

125. April 12, 2001

Night of Innocence

I had no Cow for supper –
After, took a walk –
Loved Shakespeare,
Read him, while relaxing on my spot,
Relaxing with dear Craisins, peanuts too, I had –
Shared them with a pigeon
Whose English was not bad,
Laughed at merry bicyclers
Strolled beside a walker-with-dog –
Can hardly wait
For my next taste of Hog!

126.

May 21, 2001

Past Tense

Read an article
Knit a row
Bored, bored, bored.
I know it's because
Yesterday I was not
Saved, saved, saved.
Yesterday, before communion,
'Stead of praying and fasting
I was digging into breakfast
As if it were life everlasting.
All I can say is
"Lord, please forgive,
And allow me still
Thy will to live."

127.

Sun Rising

(Cloud cover)
Lying with a
Smoky scalloped edge
Contrasting the low luminescence.
"There lies the dearest freshness
Deep down things."
Lady Moon beckoned,
Dimly,
Half-visible,
Veiled.
Now she's gone.

128. June 4, 1991

On My Birthday

Thank you for life, Lord.
Thank you for birth.
Thank you that I am on this earth.
Thank you for sunshine.
Thank you for flowers.
Help me to fill lovingly my hours.

129.   Nov. 13, 2000

Lucky

Dashing through the snow
On my good old shank's mare,
Wonder where I'll go
Could be anywhere.

Yesterday He rose –
An Easter we'll savour.
Yes, it is written He reappeared
In a more ghostly flavour.

A cake of icing sugar
Crunches 'neath my feet;
Crystal clear is the air
But lacking heat.

So home I will wend
To an inviting chair
And the warmth in my tummy
I feel sure will be there.

The Pencil

The way to start
Is to draw a line
With two important tools –
A sharp or mechanical pencil
And a Metric edge which rules.

Now you've got your start
And so make a chart.
The Rule will cross your t's so fine
That God won't see a crooked line –
You'll feel free to inflame your i's
And maybe win the Nobel Prize!

But if not, still,
Every day –
Don't just brush your hair –
Reach for this Candle of Hope instead.
Use <u>it</u> to make your prayer –
And your plan of action,

Your agenda,
What you're going to do.
Sketch the steps that lie ahead –
It takes a minute, true,
But like the draft of essays –
Like maps the sailors trust,
'Twill make your footsteps surer
T'wards your daily Crust.

131.   April 23, 2000

The sky is a myriad of cloud formations
Permeated by the spiking rays
Of the determined sun,
Like me,
Unwilling to say Adieu
To a day
Not only of Spring,
Not only Sunday,
But Easter ……..
And therefore
I understand, Sun,
Why even the truculent clouds
Can't darken you.

132.   May 6, 2003

O we thank Thee for the Blood
And we thank Thee for the mud,
And we wish that we could really speak Thy Name
On a Tuesday or a Wednesday
Or a Monday or a Saturday,
As if every day were just the same.
But Sunday is thee Holy Day
When we may talk of things
That don't relate, adhere, connect to money.
That's all the time
In this rushed world –
This land of flowing milk
And good bee's honey.

133. December 11, 1993

Prediction

Pink and clear and Bread all over
Is what I hope this Xmas is,
'Cause 'though we think of a Saviour's birth –
I wonder where He really is?

Of course He's waiting in the Heaven
Hoping to be born,
Hoping His Spirit 'til then will shine
Every Christmas morn.

Red expresses glad assurance –
Once again He's here!
Red expresses joy and
Brave unqualified cheer –

But pink is something deeper;
There's something sure in pink.
Pink is knowing that the Coming
Is realer than you think.

In spite of all my flaws of diction,
Here is my prediction:

Mankind has really progressed
Since the last great Event.
We've traveled to the Moon;
Great effort has been spent.

God will reward such effort.
The next Miracle will be
On a shelter on Mars –
I pray there'll be a tree.

We must mobilize our forces
To move in this direction –

Concert the languages
And Metric system,
<u>Net</u>work the computers;
<u>Save</u> every penny;
<u>Force</u> our kids to study hard
To stay sane through the journey;
<u>Keep</u> on hoping,
<u>Never</u> give in –
Make sure God knows which boat we're in!

<u>Love</u> our neighbours, and animals too —
<u>Think</u> hard to discover which Good to do.

And then we'll find inside ourself
Both Baby and Mother —
Angel-songs, happiness,
Love of Sister and Brother.

Christ will shine
In our own eyes
And once again be seen —
Because we've made the MENTAL EFFORT
To glorify our Green.

Each present that is given
Inspired by a Brain,
Mothered by human craft
To help Peace to reign,
Is a virgin gift to GOD
'Cause it's Love in a Box —
If it expresses thoughtfulness —
Even if it's sox —

But Red is quite de rigeur

This year too –

Cause HUBBLE'S BEEN FIXED !!!

Mary Christ MASS to You.

--oh Happy New Year, too – and many mooooooore

Last verse of "Onward Christian Soldiers"

Onward, then, ye people,

Join our happy throng.

Blend with ours your voices

In the triumph song;

Glory, laud, and honour

Unto Christ the King.

This, through countless ages, men and angels sing.

Onward, Christian soldiers,

Marching as to war.,

With the cross of Jesus going on before.